Empowerment of Self Worth

Empowerment of Self Worth

Latrice Gaddy

Contents

Welcome To My Truth About My Self-Worthiness and the Lack of Knowing It

My name is Latrice and I lived in unworthiness for over half of my life. I've been abused, abandoned, neglected, etc. I had to learn about my worthiness before I could live in it. I had to understand where it fell apart from the beginning until the present day. Authoring this book helps others that are going through or have been through the same trauma that I've experienced and remain stuck mentally. I want to help free them from that bondage.

EMPOWERMENT OF SELF WORTH

This is where my self-worthiness starts, stops, and comes back to stay!

I want to give honor to my Lord and Savior, Jesus Christ, my Pastor, Apostle Robert Parmalee, my Husband, my children, and my grandchildren. Thank you Lord; for giving me this opportunity to share my life with someone other than myself. You are so AMAZING! You make my life so much better; I can't imagine not having you in my life, so many people have left me or just don't rock with me, but you never left my side. I've never felt love the way I love you. I want to know more about you! It makes me even happier when I can dive into your world and be there for a while WOW! What a feeling it is to be able to be in your presence. I just wanted to let you know once again what and who you are to me; THANK YOU, FATHER, GOD!!!

I didn't know about my worthiness for half of my life. I ran away from my family when I got old enough to do so but just because I was old enough doesn't mean I was ready. I was raised with a bunch of alcoholics and drug addicts. I was taught to signify with other family members, to talk about family members behind their backs and to make fun of the "Bible totters" (and now I'm one)! I was taught to fight my family members, that it's ok to help outsiders before you help your own people, to neglect, to be abusive and the list goes on. I was taught all these things before I left my foundation of growth. WOW! I was surely on my way to self-destruction. Going out into the real world with these kinds of tools was a definite set up for failure. I knew nothing about what I was worth and all the tools that were given to me made me find my worthiness that much harder. When you leave your foundation, you should have some sense of your self-worthiness, if not all of it. It begins at home: you should learn how to be kind, and loving even when it's hard; have some self-control about yourself, and never let someone else take your worthiness away from you. You are important to yourself and if you have breath in you that means you are important to God! And that's what you should have your focus on. When you know and understand your worth, you don't allow anything in your life. I'm worthy of being listened to, of a gentle touch, of a conversation and of RESPECT. I'm worthy in all areas of my life.

Tell yourself this daily and believe it!

Let me tell you about my destructive way of living before I started to understand how worthy I am. When I was younger in grade school I struggled with my reading. I always had to go to a separate class with some other students because we were at a lower level than the rest of the class. Students would always make jokes or just laugh at us, which made us defensive and incredibly angry, shy, closed-off and so alone. I use to fight all the time in grade school; I got that from my family. We fought in the home as well as outside. It was mostly women in the family and no real men were there to protect us or lead us in any positive way of living. In high school my English teacher would call on me to read out loud and I would get so mad at him. It's like he knew I couldn't read on a level of the grade I was in. I would get nervous, my whole body would shake and shiver, my words would shake as I would try to get them out of my mouth. I was a first-year student because Lord knows I couldn't get any further with that type of embarrassment. That was the final decision about High School for me at that moment. I played the "I'm sick" role for a while until I realized I didn't have to. My grandmother would mention something about me going to school but it wasn't a big deal. I worked at the airport as a security guard on check point, making $3.75 an hour (back then that was a lot of money to be making). Man, I thought I was doing ok until my mother and step dad started asking for the money I was making. I had to pay some bills; which wouldn't have been a problem if it had been explained how I was getting prepared for the real world. Nothing was really explained, it was more "Do what I say and don't ask me no damn questions' . I inflicted this same dysfunction onto my children; unbeknownst to their way of living and if I could take it back I would. I remember that my little sister said to me after I had my son: "Why don't you buy yourself some shoes worth having?" You deserve to get yourself nice quality things." I was still shopping at Payless at the time, because that's all I was taught to buy. Once my youngest sister said that to me; I started to think "she makes a lot of sense" but no matter how much sense she was making, I didn't see or feel what she was saying to me until some time later and started to do things a little different for myself. Having low self-esteem was taking over and living from the inside out of my body. I used to be so ashamed to engage in a conversation or any type of setting that had anything to do with reading because it would make me look and feel foolish to not know. I was drowning and I had to figure out how to swim, I wanted this feeling to be over and I was only at the forefront of the beginning of it all. I hid underneath my embarrassment because of what I didn't know, too ashamed to ask for help. You feel that when your family lets you down everyone will let you down until it's proven otherwise. I taught myself many things over the years and the one thing that'll always stick with me is that you should love yourself before you try loving anyone else... I've enrolled myself in many different programs trying to get my GED and every one of them was an epic failure. I've been in more relationships than I want to talk about. I was chasing a fantasy without knowing what kind of fantasy I was chasing. I was looking for love and didn't understand the coordination of love, being in love, being loved or just being in a committed relationship. How was I supposed to make it/this work when I knew nothing about it? Man; I was on a road leading me right back to where it all started, not realizing what lies ahead of me, no warning, with my eyes wide open!

<u>**When People Show You Who They Are, You Better Believe Them; That First Time Right In That Moment...**</u>

They don't change no matter how much you see some good in them. See them for who they present themselves to be!

I met my children's father and when I tell you I ran right into the DANGER ZONE! That's exactly what I mean. That man flipped my world all the way around and around and around again. I wasn't ready for the games he had in mind to play on me, I was a player without my own acknowledgment of the game (this is another story to tell)! I can and will tell you I loved this man more than I ever loved myself at that time; which was and is ALWAYS the wrong thing to do. I lost myself and even more, I lost my self-worth being in such a relationship/marriage. I learned later, almost towards the end of the marriage, that he and his friends and some family members had a bet about who would get me first if at all. WOW! Imagine learning that you were nothing but a freaking bet on someone you loved more than you loved yourself. When I tell you it's very important for you to do your work; learn how to fall in love with yourself after you fall in love with Jesus! It's Very Important... This relationship/marriage could have taken me out, but God picks his toughest soldiers for his hardest tasks. Thank you Lord for holding my hand through the worst part of my life! I'm nothing without you! Thank You Jesus.

AND THIS IS WHERE IT ALL STARTED

My family didn't support me with my education. They actually made fun of the fact that I couldn't read as they did with everyone who couldn't read or write in the family. I have always wondered why my family never helped their own people, those with whom they share bread. It's still like that to this day, some things never change I guess. I remember when I was about seven, maybe nine, my mom asked me to read something to her.; I stumbled over every word on that paper. My mother never got me any help, and I never knew how damaging it was going to be against my self-worthiness throughout the years to come. It took more away from me at that moment than I could have ever imagined. Knowing how to read and comprehend what you're reading is very powerful and it'll build your confidence (because not knowing makes you have no confidence trust me) as well as add to your self-worthiness. We never sat down and had conversations about emotions and how important they are as part of your life. I didn't know how to express my emotions without being aggressive. I was once told my emotions were all over the place (sometimes dealing with certain people brings out different, if not all emotions) I heard what was said, but at that moment I got defensive. I've tried to have conversations with anyone that made my emotions change but I just didn't know how to carry the conversation without being aggressive.

In my family, being aggressive was the only way of expressing your-self. I learned later in life that being aggressive would turn a lot of people away from you. I thought it was a cultural thing, meaning all blacks speak this way. This is what I was taught from the root of my being. BOY was I wrong. Not everyone in my culture, just in my family. I had to learn how to talk without being so aggressive. I had to learn how to be more patient with myself. Learning a different way of life could be exhausting but liberating as well.

I love that God teaches me everything that I know; God has his ways of letting me know what he's always saying. I'm filled with the Holy Spirit and I thank you Jesus for that; because without it I would still be lost.

I always knew I was different from the family I was born in. I wasn't born to fit in, I was born to shine! As I got older and really started seeing things for myself, I started to speak about it to my oldest sister, who made my life a living hell.

My oldest sister and I never got along. She was a real live WITCH! She never had a real genuine love for me. She really was a bully to me, tried to boss me around and make me do all the things she didn't want to do. We would have to clean up every day while my mother was at work and she would make my oldest brother and I do all the things she didn't want to do. My oldest sister didn't know how to be nice to me and in our younger years she taught me nothing good until I got to be a mother and out on my own. She would treat me and my friends like dirt but I was to respect her and her friends. I always looked up to my sister. She never would give me the time of day and would take my cousin with her everywhere, she would talk, laugh and play around with him. All the time he was my favorite out of the whole family.

MAN, I MISS HIM!! R.I.P COUSIN...

You know older sisters show you the way of life in a sense; right? Well, all she wanted to do was boss me around and tell me I was fast, and I didn't listen to her. My mother didn't teach us how to not fight each other, to be there for each other, or love and support each other. She never told us to not let anyone from the outside or inside (sometimes) come between us. I guess that's because she didn't get the love and support from her siblings, she couldn't teach it to her kids and we lack that to this day in this family.

To be listened to is to be talked to. You can't yell and cuss and call others out of their names and expect them to not give it back to you.

My mother worked Monday - Friday while my oldest sister, my oldest brother, and myself stayed at the house with my grandmother and her kids, my aunts, uncles and ALL their friends. I remember it being hell living there. My aunts were so mean that they yelled, cussed us out, called us names just made us feel less than others. My sister would fight them with my mom as if she was my mom's protector at the time. I was so young that it was scary until I got used to it.

That's exactly where my sister got, being so mean almost to the point of being a bully. She still have these ways to this day and can't see how living in that place for so long has damaged her/us. I tried to build a relationship with my sister as grown women, but it's so much damage there. It takes two people to build a relationship and when one is not in a season of self-reflection it's almost impossible.

I'm growing, I'm listening to God, And I'm always available.

My self-reflection is everything to me and if I must cut people off, then I must cut people off. It doesn't mean I don't have love for people. I'm on a personal journey and my sister has her own demons to fight, as do I.

My oldest brother and I started off with a rocky relationship. He choked me when I was about five, I thought I was going to die and I thought he was crazy. He was chasing my oldest sister and my youngest aunt while they were babysitting me on a Saturday morning, while mom was shopping. He couldn't catch them, so he grabbed me. He was always mad and mean. Maybe they (my siblings) were so mean because of how we got treated by our aunts and uncles. Now, I can say my aunt's and uncle's got the same treatment from their aunt's and uncle's. I was able to see my great aunt's and great uncle's and had a relationship with them before they were called home. I guess the apple doesn't fall very far from the tree at all. My brother didn't get the love or education he needed either, we were some lost souls trying to find our way; getting into everything that would take us down even more. Wow! The things that damages you from your own rooted foundation.

Knowledge is power! I'm trying so hard to be better today than yesterday; I'm listening to you God!

I have a younger sister and a younger brother. I tried to be there for my younger siblings as much as I knew how but I didn't realize running away from my demons would leave an impact on the ones I left behind. They're doing a lot better than I am these days and from the outside looking in, one of them for sure seems to have it together. I know at some point my younger sister looked up to me until she had to start watching me live my mother's life in a different, yet, same life. That's what happened when your foundation was one of the weakest links that could have ever been around. She builds her own village outside of the family and I know that her soul gets weak and that she wishes her own family foundation could be as strong as her village foundation. I know she struggles just as hard, if not harder, that we are so widely spreaded out from each other. Our family consists of this group sitting here, this group sitting over there and you better believe that if someone from a different group goes to visit the next group, when you leave, you are being talked about and you can feel it from the moment you turn around to leave or maybe even while you're standing there trying to be a part of their group for the moment. It makes you not believe in yourself when your own family puts you down and doesn't notice your weaknesses. It's not a way to help you but to tear you down. Running isn't always the solution or maybe not the solution at all. You can and will run into danger on your running journey. You'll be trapped there for years or so and God will bring you right back to that very thing you ran from until you can get the lesson that's in it for you.

I made so many mistakes along this journey called life. Until I got on the road of self-reflection, I was lost, mean, confused, and just a hot mess. I carried all this baggage into my kid's life and didn't realize I was damaging their state of being until it was almost too late (that's another story to tell).

My youngest brother was my son before I had my own son two years after my brother was born. My mom was forty years old when she had my youngest brother and was determined to have him at any cost, it seemed like that at that moment in time. I kept my youngest brother and took him pretty much everywhere I went until I started dating my first husband. I got pregnant early in this so-called relationship (I'll get into details about this relationship/Marriage in another story). I didn't get to spend more than those two years with my youngest brother before we had to take off and move three hours away, which was a lot for me. I was still young, dumb and naïve. I had never moved away from my family before, but I was ready to go in my mind as I had nothing to lose and everything to gain. Boy was I wrong!

When we moved from the family building (finally) it was different because we left with no real tools to be successful in life, meaning my siblings and I were set up for failure from our own roots., You expect love and respect coming from someone who was not taught to be loved or respected on a regular basis (Lord, please help us).

This book is to introduce you to how Empowerment of Self Worth was born for me. I always thought my first husband was the cause of all my sadness and unhappiness but if I'm going to be honest about my life; I have to tell the whole entire truth and my sadness, pain, abandonment, neglect, abuse all started from the root of my foundation, which is my family, the people I ran away from at the beginning of it all.

As life went on and my destruction got worse I felt like I was at the bottom of the ocean with my eyes wide open and I needed to get out, I needed to be free, I had to figure out how to get out of there.

I remember one day while working at Meijer's in the jewelry department. This Caucasian woman (a customer) started a conversation
with me and that conversation was the change of my life. She talked
to me about some of her problems as well as listened to some of my
problems and asked me if I'd ever read the book "The Purpose-Driven
Life" before. I told her "No I haven't even heard of it, I don't think".
We finished our conversation, she gave me some advice then she left.
As I was waiting on another customer, I look up and here she comes
with the book "The Purpose-Driven Life".

I was excited, in disbelief, warm-hearted and had so many emotions
going on in that moment, but I also was ready to get the work started.
I was at the bottom of the sea and ready to come up for some air.

I took that book home and once I started diving into it I couldn't put
it down. I was in awe! I wanted more and more. I began to learn so
much. I started to change how I ate. I used to drink Pepsi all day long
and would wake up in the middle of the night for a Pepsi which isn't
good for anyone, to be honest. I started feeling better once I traded
my Pepsi for water and before I knew it, I wasn't drinking Pepsi
anymore. WOW! Life is changing already. This was just the beginning
of my spiritual and self-reflection journey, this was back in 2003 and
I'm still on that journey. I've learned so many things about myself, my
family, my children, and my full circle. I've lost people whom I
thought were important to me, and I've gained confidence within the
loss; knowing my well-being is so much more important than people
really helping me along the way. God will provide good people in my
life, is what I kept telling myself, over and over. God already has it
worked out for me; I had and still have work to do. I'm so grateful for
another chance to get it right.

Over the years I've become a Woman of God, I've gotten my High
School diploma, I've gotten my Business Accountant Certificate, I've
gotten my Life Coach Certificate, and I'm writing Books so I guess I
can say I'm an Author! I've gotten remarried, I'm reconnecting with
my children building better and stronger bonds. I'm so excited about
what God is doing in my life.

Praise God! I'm nothing without you Jesus...

We go through things in life without understanding of what it means, how we are supposed to handle situations. In life, you need tools; tools for every obstacle that comes your way. Honesty is needed; you need to be honest with yourself about everything. If you're not honest with yourself, how can you determine if someone else is being honest with you? Everything starts within yourself. Be kind to yourself, and love yourself always. If you can't figure out how to love yourself, I would advise you to start doing self-reflection work and I guarantee you, you'll find all the answers and so much more. There's healing there, there's change there, there's growth there.

Let's learn about SHIP. Well, the definition of a SHIP is a vessel larger than a boat for transporting people or goods by sea.

Most times when you get in a commitment with someone you establish a SHIP: friendship, relationship, partnership, MARRIAGE, brothers, sisters and fellowship. Now when the ship on the sea is transporting all the goods, they are very careful, and cautious, that they take their time, and above all, they make sure everything is good to go before they move across the sea for travel. This is exactly how we must handle our SHIPS in our lives. We must take the time for every one of our SHIPS that's in our lives; starting with the SHIP we have with GOD! We must make sure he's first because if he's first everything else will fall into place. We must have an understanding as to what order God wants us to move in, how God wants us to move, and how our thought process should be; once the thought process is in order then, we start working on what comes out of our mouth. Making sure you're speaking in a way that's pleasing to God. We can accomplish anything in this world through our Lord and Savior Jesus Christ! Starting with God is the very beginning.

Always remember, you are no good for anyone if you don't get yourself into a relationship with God; so, he can teach you all about yourself. Once you get that understanding you need from God about yourself, you're unstoppable.

It's time for us women to live in our worthiness. It's time for us to understand where we lost our worth and how we get it back and how we continue to live in it without losing it again.

Empower yourself to be better than you were yesterday, to think differently, to be a better wife, a better Mother, friend, and sister. Empower yourself into your self-worth!

This is an important tool that we must use daily for ourselves and for each other; lift your sister up if you see her down or broken in any way at all, it will make you feel just as good if not better to just lift her up!

From me to you, you are the most amazing person that you will ever meet. You are most important to yourself first. You are powerful in your own right so make sure you show up for yourself always!

EMPOWERMENT OF SELF-WORTH!

The motivation for me is knowing that there's someone out there just like me, just like I was stuck in a situation not knowing who I was, loving someone more than I loved myself, having low self-esteem, no confidence in myself, not knowing how to read and felt very misunderstood. I didn't have the help or the tools to come out of this dark way of living, thinking, and speaking until I took the road of self-finding. I didn't know what to expect but I was willing to deal with whatever I was about to see and because I went down that self-finding journey, I'm able to understand that everything isn't what its surface shows (meaning, what you see is not what you always get).

Most of the time the issues are deeper than we want to go. I've learned when someone is having a conversation with me and I hear a word that's hurtful or maybe even true to my well-being, to not get so angry and hurt with the words that I'm hearing but listen to everything that's being said. We must have a clear understanding of what is being said and why it's being said before we can respond. Sometimes the words that you hear about yourself repeatedly over the years are the very words that play over and over in your head telling you what you're not and how WORTHLESS you are.

We must reach deep down within ourselves to understand the power that lies within us!

I strive to empower women who are stuck in that situation, here and now, there is hope!

Naive, abused, abandoned, neglected, lost, uneducated, misunderstood, used, stepped on, spit on, no confidence, low self-esteem, unloved -

This was me when I didn't know myself and this is how I lost my self-worth.

This is who I was before I knew whom I belonged to, what I'm here to do, why I'm here on this earth in this world doing exactly what it is that God called me to do, and right when he called me to get it all done… I'm right where God wants me to be in this present moment.

These are the steps I had to take. Over and over until I understood the assignment.

Joshua: - 1:9:

"Have I not commanded you? Be strong and courageous, do not be afraid; do not be discouraged, for the Lord your God will be with you wherever you go."

Proverbs: - 3:6:

"Seek his will in all you do, and he will show you which path to take."

Prayer:

O Father, I love being in your presence and soaking up the peace and love you have for me. I want what you want for me because I know it's the very best - In Jesus' mighty name. Amen.

- Our future is filled with hope but if we are going to face our future, we must face our fears
- God will give you a task that will blow your mind. Did you hear what I said?
- You can sit in a situation and be trying to understand how did I get here? The answer is : lean not on your own understanding! When you be still and connect with God, when you align your life with God and get a relationship with him is when he (God) will start to give you some understanding of this world.

Prayer:

Lord, I trust you with my future, I'm done fixating on all that could go wrong, and I'm ready to trust that you have filled my future with hope. I'm looking forward to my future knowing that whatever comes, you are already there. I'm ready to walk boldly forward into you for me! In Jesus' mighty name. Amen.

Romans 8:28:

"And we know that in all things God works for the good of those who love him, who have been called according to his purpose."

"God lavishes us with love" (1 John 3:1).

"God is all-knowing" (John 3:20).

"God is loving and wants only good for us" (Psalm: 86:15).

"God works things out for our good" (Romans 8:28).

"God is with us" (Deuteronomy 3:16).

"God is our helper" (Isaiah 41:10).

"And no one can thwart his plans" (Isaiah 14:27).

Prayer:

Lord, expose the lies the enemy has been telling me about me. Help me to see you rightly as trustworthy and good. When I begin to doubt, remind me that you are with me. I trust that you are good at being the Lord of my life through the highs and lows. In Jesus' mighty name. Amen.

- The feeling inside of you is God calling you to a new adventure, to grow to a higher level of understanding, to a better future.
- Standing strong means getting out of your own way and letting God work in and through you.
- Don't focus on the reason: "I can't". Focus on the God that can.

- We've settled for loss instead of celebrating our dreams and gifts.
- God will give you everything you need in order to do what he calls you to do.
- When we talk to God seriously, we learn to take ourselves seriously.
- Lean not on your own understanding.

Romans: 8:6 :

"The mind governed by the flesh is death but the mind governed by the spirit is life and peace."

Sometimes God wants us to go right but we think we have it all figured out and the very thing God is telling us to do, we do the opposite. That's when we start to live our life with discomfort, things start spinning out of control and we don't have a clue as to why. If we don't get ourselves aligned with God; we're going to always have discomfort in ourselves and our lives as well.

I want to empower women who are not afraid to receive empowerment from another woman! It takes a woman who understands herself knowing that she/I can't do this alone. This thing requires help!

Release, Reflect, Renew, Regain, Renounce....

Become what you're called to do and discover your who, when, why, and what! If you're willing to do the work and ready to uncover your worthiness,- "The Empowerment Of Self–Worth" is here and available to you. You will go on this journey of self-reflection and the result will be filled with power, knowledge, wisdom, and understanding of this world.

Your self-worth is so important to yourself!

Free yourself ! It's time!

Your inner-self is crying out for help unlock the door and let Freedom in - you won't be disappointed...

We don't transform in just one day or without effort but it all starts with us.

When we are blinded by our own concerns, we become limited to a narrow awareness of the world.

We must remember that God gives us all the understanding we need, all we must do is ask God to free our minds of our own thoughts, and keep us still while he's doing the work for us! Then and only then will we rejoice in our lives. Align yourself with God's plan for your life.

These are just some of the steps/things I did and still are doing to this day for the rest of my life.

If it wasn't for you Father, God!

When you are drowning in your own self-pity, you feel like the world is against you. You want out, you want help from whatever it is that's got you down in the dumpster. You want people to say the right thing that relates to your situation in hopes that they will have the answer to your problem, that they will have the understanding that would set me free from this disaster of a life that I'm living.

BEING LOST

I came from the bottom of the barrel and literally crawled my way to some sort of air, light and freshness. Once I got a little bit of air; I then had to learn how to swim. You see, being at that bottom I had to learn how to do everything that had anything to do with life; because I had no tools and nowhere to go. I had nowhere to go; because I ran from that place, that place of loneliness. When I was there, I had no one I could really depend on, and they could be there for me and teach me how to live in my own skin. I watched my cousin get the best education/training from his mom and his dad and when I would be curious about what or how to do what they were doing,; my aunt and her son's father made me leave from there, I couldn't stand there and just get the same learning as he was getting I had to get away. Get away to do what? I had nothing to do other than pick on the other elders in the house because that's what I was taught to do. picking with the elders that was ok to be around, but I couldn't be around learning time. If that's not dysfunctional, you tell me what it is? I didn't understand that then; but today I come to understand that the household was being run by strong but weak women. I watched the women in my family fight the wrong way for the majority of my life. When you fight bitterness and anger in your heart you lose out on life. Anger is another form of bondage that holds you in one spot and keeps you from thinking rationally. I was there for years! For so many years of my life, I was in bondage called the silence of the mind at one point I felt like my mind couldn't go any further, this was it I was doomed for a lifetime of the silence of the mind; it had been taking away from me and I was drowning in my overloaded mind that had become silenced. I became destructive in every area of my life. You see if you were around me you were a target; a target to be taken down. I couldn't see past all the wrong that was in my life. I thought everyone was against me. This is what happens when your mind is lost and all over the place. This was no way to live. I had to get out of that bondage way of living and thinking and figure out how to live in reality.

Have you ever been there; in a silence of the mind bondage? It's like the thoughts are there but you can't articulate or put them in any perspective of your own.

Are you there, right now in your life today?

I broke away from my family because I wasn't enough for them in my own skin; as I raised my children, I find myself breaking away from them because I feel sometimes, I'm just not enough; only this time the pain is more severe. I gave my children everything I thought they needed in life and more, but sometimes I feel like I'm just not enough. I've always asked God to help me with the obsession of love that I have for my children because I wasn't getting the same kind of love and understanding as they became older and into adulthood. It is especially important that you know and understands who you are giving yourself to; let only bear children with. As a union, you build your children together as one on the same alignment, the alignment that was intended for us by God. I gave my children to God an exceptionally long time ago; I trust his will be done for their lives. When God is ready to give them back to me, he will! Until then, I'll be obedient to his leadership over my life.

I'm learning how to swim all on my own.

I am enough for God!!

Every time I get in this place, this place of the silence of the mind; God has to come in and rescue me from my own self. If God doesn't come to rescue me, I'll be stuck there for only God knows when. I am incredibly grateful for God giving me the knowledge and understanding that if I don't call on him when I recognize that I'm slipping into darkness it could be detrimental to my health. Thank You Jesus!

I didn't tell my family about a lot of the things I was experiencing while I was away with my first husband. I never thought they cared deeply enough about me to share that dark side of my life. I didn't want war, I wanted solutions. I wanted to become better, not to get out to become nothing and do nothing with my life. I've always wanted more; I just didn't know how to go about making things happen for me until I had to learn how to do it all on my own.

Have you ever gone through the I should a, could a, would a: kind of season in your life? If so, it might not be the last season you'll experience if you don't know to whom you belong.

I had this friend at one season in my life. She was a dope Fien and a booster. She had her own apartment; she was different from me; I didn't do any drugs I was afraid of what it would make me look like and I always wanted to be looked upon as a young lady into a woman and nothing less. We were friends for a few years, I think she was more into my brother than me; of course, I couldn't do the things he would do with her and didn't want to. She would do her dope in front of me and would say to me: "Don't you ever do this shit, you hear me"? One time we were sitting in the car waiting to go see her uncle who was in the hospital, so she could take him some dope too. She did hers while we were in the car; the minute she did it, she held her head back and tears started to run down her face for no reason whatsoever. My eyes got big; I believe I was in a state of shock at the time. I remember saying to myself she doesn't never has to worry about that, cause if it's doing that to her there's no telling what it'll do to me. I'm good, FOREVER!

I was lost, not desperate. Well, not desperate in that way. I was lost and desperate for love.

There are many ways you can be lost in life. Most of the time we don't know our self-worth, so we accept just about anything that comes our way; which is usually unhealthy for us across the board.

Being lost in the world usually starts of being hurt, ugly, angry, and hopeless. If we could just get a hold of ourselves before we slip into something we can't get out of. If we could just understand that our mind and body are about to go through something so we could inter-ject it all together and move forward to the next chapter/season of our lives, but no. That's not what God wanted for us. Think about it! If God doesn't put us in a lost state of mind; then the majority of us won't even connect with him. So, you see! We must experience some seasons of our lives lots; so that God can start the work within us.

SELF REFLECTION!

EMPOWERMENT OF SELF-WORTH...

BEING ILLITERATE

This was me for thirty years of my life. I say thirty because that's when I started checking into my worth; that's when it really started to matter that I couldn't read, and I wanted to do something about it. I knew I couldn't pronounce certain words or even know what they meant; so, a lot of times I was reading stuff and making up what I thought the word said and meant; then tried to use what I made up to be meaningful making myself look and feel more uncomfortable. Man, I had a lot to teach myself and a very long way to go. I first had to learn how to stop being so mad at everybody because they left me out here to figure this thing called life out all by myself. You're here now, what are you going to do?

I used to shy away from any and every uncomfortable situation that had anything to do with reading. Living this way, in hiding was so lonely. I was afraid to let people know my disability of not being a part of normalcy in life; because knowing how to read and comprehend what you're reading OMG! It's powerful and it gets you very far in life. I know because I've been on both ends of it.

I watched my family take care of and help outsiders become very successful and would degrade me as if I wasn't their own blood.

Imagine That! I've been suffering from anger most of my life. I started marriage in anger; in anger at my family not wanting me, so I accepted the next worse lesson of my life, my first husband. Big Mistake. BIG! HUGE! He knew I couldn't read but that was more ammunition to use against me, to play mind games with me, this was perfect for him, after all, I was just a bet to him anyway; to make me feel less than, was nothing to him. I would shy away from it at all costs.

I was bringing children into the world with this thing I was carrying on my shoulders for years. I wasn't feeling complete, and I was tired of hiding behind my shame; I wanted to do something about it, I wanted to make a difference in my life, and I wanted to be a role model for my children in a good life. I've always seen myself being more than what I was doing; I never really understood what my task was until I started connecting with God.

I would shy away from certain jobs because they would ask for too many credentials and I didn't have them, which made me feel even worse; so, I asked my cousin to give me a diploma until I could get mines. I would be scared to let people into my world; I was so ashamed of myself that I couldn't allow people to come in and make fun of me. I knew what I was capable of because of the anger that was living inside of me and the way I was raised, I didn't mind getting my hands dirty; so, I stayed to myself and cried out to God and listened to Whitney Houston at the same time. Being illiterate kept me from meeting fabulous and outstanding people because you are what you attract and I'm amazing, I just didn't know just how amazing I was while I was sitting in illiteracy.

I used to always have my oldest sister take care of all my important business for me because I just couldn't do it. I didn't really understand a lot of things that I was reading, and she was savvy in that way; she knew how to get around and figure things out. I trusted her until she started telling me 'You can do this yourself. Why don't you ever do this, it's easy? It may have been easy for her; however, it was terrifying for me. I didn't really know my way around many places; even though

I lived in the city of Chicago and was born and raised there, I just didn't really know. I didn't have confidence because I knew I didn't have the education I needed; I didn't feel smart. I would ask my youngest Aunt to help me with some directions. Sometimes I would have to meet my first husband at the Military Ball, and I needed help with the directions, and she was the one around this time that I could get help from. She yelled at me and was saying "Come on now P-Lady, you act like you don't understand what I'm saying" and to be honest, I didn't. I just couldn't really comprehend the directions. I just dug myself a hole that I could live in and not just so my illiteracy to anyone else, but that was just wishful thinking. It was always there, and I didn't know how to live in it at the time, so I ran and ran until I couldn't run anymore.

I remember one time I was in the car with my first husband; we were coming from somewhere for the military and he needed a check to be written. He asked me to get his checkbook out and I didn't realize that he wanted me to fill the check out, so I get it out to give to him and he said fill it out for me. My body started to sweat, I was shaking, and I didn't want him to see this in me, I figured he knew; he would always play mind games to see where you are, and I always felt less than when he would do this to me. So, I had to write Santa Fe and I couldn't spell it for the life of me. I felt so ashamed of myself at that moment, and I knew I had to do something about it, I just hadn't figured it out yet.

As time went on, I would try to keep myself away from anything that had to do with exposing the fact that I was not good at reading and sometimes writing.

I remember when I first got interested in reading chapter books. It was my ex-husband that asked me if I had ever read this book called "Milk in My Coffee" before. I thought he was being funny at first, he knew I struggled with reading, I didn't want to deny the fact that I was interested in reading the book. I truly didn't want him to know from my mouth to his ears, because he just wasn't the type to help you in your weakness, but make you feel even more ashamed of your shortcomings in life. I told him of course, I want to read the book. I kept telling myself, I can do this, I can finish this entire book on my own, when I get stuck on a word, I'll just look it up and take my time with punctuation and pronouncing any word I come across, you can do this, you will do this. I took a chance, and I started reading that book and couldn't put it down. I was impressed with myself. I wanted more and more of not only the book but the way I was researching words and getting a better understanding of what I was reading and what the meaning of words were, was blowing my mind and building me up at the same time. I was intrigued by this new tool that I have taught myself, and it was working for me.

I kept this inside for so many years. I didn't want people to know that I struggle with this one important part of my life, that could and would take me very far in life. When you shy away from the world because of your shortcomings in life, you are only hurting yourself, and making your healing process longer than it needs to be. Find someone you can trust and confide in so you can get the correct tools that you need.

Have you ever kept something that's important for your health or well-being away from everyone else?

Are you living in that space today?

How long are you willing to suffer?

You should always make a conscious decision on the way you're going to show up for yourself. You are important to you first. How can you be there for anyone else if you're weak in mind, body, and spirit?

Education is very important. Don't ever be afraid to ask for help when needed. Do not put yourself in bondage that you'll have to sit in for years or so because you have become too stuck and confused to get out of it. People prey to the weak and take advantage of them and leave them for the dead. Make something out of your life.

Through it all, God has always been with me. I just didn't realize it until I started crying out to him and he started showing me who I am and what I'm made of.

I was so ashamed of myself, yet afraid to say I was struggling. I was only making life, and situations more complicated for myself. It was killing me inside along with other things I choose to hide from myself, and everyone else too.

BEING A MILITARY WIFE

There were so many parts to being a military wife. You become one; you get benefits just as they do. Military wives have their own community; they stick together help one another out and are always there for support. Being a military wife, you need as much support as you can get; you're away from your loved ones and it's like being in a foreign country. You build a foundation of your own if you can. I was a military wife for ten years and every one of those years I knew nothing that I was privy to know. My first husband made sure he kept me away from any and everything about the military, he kept me from the wives because there was a lot of information that those wives could've and would've given me. Had that happened I could've left much earlier than I did. Information is POWER, I would've had all the tools I needed to be free from him.

I found out later that my children and I had been traveling around the country with no life insurance; but my ex-husband was fully insured. I wouldn't have known this if his baby sister hadn't told me. One day we were sitting and discussing insurance and I said how I didn't have to worry because we were fully covered, and she looked at me and said "With who?". I said "The Marines" and that's when she told me that the military doesn't insure the family, just those that are in the military that she had to get outside insurance for her two boys. My face turned so red; I was burning on the inside; I was so darn mad; another lie that fell on me and my children. Had I been part of the wife's club in the Military I would've known this at the beginning of the marriage.

I remember when my ex-husband wanted to purchase a building for his so-called friend, but he couldn't do it without me being a part of it, I had to sign the papers with him as his wife. I didn't want to do it; I told him no. What about buying a house for us? He had his baby sister beg me to do this for him, at the time she and I had become good friends (I thought)! She was already in the Military, and I honestly thought she was giving me good advice, I found out that she is just as dark as he was, and she was not to be trusted anymore.

Being in the Military you get moved around a lot. During this move we were in separate cars when we got to the new house and was having a conversation with the landlord and she told me, "Your niece called to tell me you guys were pulling up to the place". In my mind, I was like "What niece?". After that I talked to my ex-husband about what the landlord told me. Of course, he denied it. I kept asking who on earth could that have been. I found out later that it was another woman. It was one of his sister's boyfriend's nieces who was married at the time. She and I had a few words over the telephone in front of his family.

My friend used to come and visit me all the time. This friend, my ex-husband, couldn't stand her guts because she knew how dirty he was. He was sleeping with one of our other friends. One time my friend was at the house and my ex-husband tried to hook her up with one of his friends. She got so mad; she called me at work and told me what was going on at the house and I was livid and in disbelief. He had no shame for all the foolishness he caused it just went on and on.

There was this time when my ex got himself in some trouble while in the military. I had no clue to anything he had going on. He made sure he kept me away from anything that had to do with him. Yes! You heard me right! He was going back and forth to court and I kept asking "What's going on ?" But I would get nothing from him. He would sit outside and have conversations with his lawyer and wouldn't discuss anything with me. So, this time he had to go to court in California and he said he'll be back the next day. Well, the next day came and went; still nothing I'm getting worried about now, so I called his office and talked to one of the workers. The worker asked me "You don't know what's going on, do you?". I said my husband told me he'll be home yesterday and I haven't heard from him. The worker told me that I would have to talk to the CO (commanding officer). The CO called me and told me that my husband had signed a deal and he had been in the bricks for thirty days. I couldn't believe what I was hearing. He just left us here like this and told me nothing! I cried like a baby. I had no idea what I was going to do. I had to leave my kids in the house by themselves. I worked nights, I would panic at work when I would call home, and no one would answer the phone. I would ask my supervisor if I could leave and go check on my kids. Thank God he said yes! We were cool like that.

One time my ex-husband took the credit card from me, knowing we didn't have food and we needed some household goods for the house. I had to call one of his superiors in charge. He made him give me the card back and told him if he ever took it again, he would be in some deep trouble.

Moving from place to place can be a strain on the family, mostly the wives and the children. It becomes the playground for the husbands; they get to leave you home and explore the town without the family, and that could be good in some sense, if you had a straightforward husband who looks out for the good of his family and looks for activities to do with the family, then that's what we need, but if you're using it for your own gain and satisfaction, then you're setting yourself and your family members up for failure. This was one of the biggest problems in my first marriage, he used his job and the qualifications of the job to his advantage to stay away from us and build something elsewhere. When he did return home to us it was like living in a war zone just to have a conversation. Never could get anything real out of him. I began to zone out every time he would start a fancy island conversation that he lived on by himself because the things that came out of his mouth made no sense. I wanted to get up and walk away from this nonsense of a conversation but to do that is to be disrespectful and would cause more chaotic situations.

I always thought the children would adapt to any move that we had to make, I thought it would have been easy for them to make new friends at such a young age, and BOY! Was I wrong! It tore them apart unbeknownst to me. I found out later in life that they hated the fact that they had to leave their friends behind and try to make new ones all over again. They asked me "Do you know how hard it was not to make new friends?". My heart dropped. I missed the mark on that. I asked myself, did I not communicate well with them? Was I too far in the survivor mode to see this?

Going on family vacations is a way to bond with each other, everyone has a chance to release, reflect, rejoice, and renounce. Family, and time with your family brings on strength that's needed in every family, and these days and times it lacks the most. You must take some time while dating and getting to know one another. If it's hard to communicate with someone, before you build a family you must build a strong communication system because if you don't, you're setting your family as well as yourself up for destruction.

I didn't understand what I was getting into being a military wife. I trusted what my husband at the time was telling me. Not knowing he was filling me up with a bunch of lies that sometimes became our reality. He was my husband, this was his career, and he had better understanding of it than I did, he's been doing it for years, why wouldn't I believe him? The one true answer to that question is because I didn't know who he really was, from the soul of him, our relationship was built on nothing but lies and deceit.

We gave life to two souls, we were in denial about who we were as individuals and the souls that we created together unhealed were suffering from our own mi's haves in life. All I'm saying is I took my children on this journey of being a military wife with no knowledge of what that consists of. I took a chance, so they took the chance with me, I suffered so they suffered with me. All the time I thought I was hiding my pain I was inflicting it on them. I'M SO SORRY CHILDREN OF MINE! For I only wanted to bring peace and harmony to your life. Please forgive me.I thought I was protecting my children; I came to understand some of my decisions that were made, took me from being protective to being inflictive and in the moment, you don't realize that's what you're doing. Try to be more aware of your actions and what comes out of your mouth, it's very important to your children's health and lifetime here on earth.

When becoming a part of anything in life especially involving children make sure you do all the research possible, know what you are getting yourself into and where it could take you and your family. If there's any doubt what's so ever, research the doubt, go to your higher power and ask for some guidance along the way, be still and wait for your instructions. If you try and figure it out on your own, you'll be right back where you started at the beginning.

I was under the impression that being a military wife meant I was entitled to what he was entitled to, meaning if he gets the eye laser surgery, I can too. We have the same insurance, why couldn't I? I was always told that I couldn't with no explanation as to why, only it's not for you, you can't get what I get. I can't see just like you can't see, we're under the same insurance; make it make sense, please? And all I would ever get was "NO, YOU CAN'T. YOU'RE NOT IN THE MILITARY". Then he would tell me that I was just jealous of him. I asked, how can I be jealous of you, I'm proud of you and all your accomplishments, I just would like to be a part of celebrating them with you. He told me "Yeah, right! You're just jealous as if he needed something to fight with me about". This became a normal saying in the home now, it went on so long I start to ask myself, am I jealous of him? The only thing I could ever come up with is, why would I be jealous of him? With his ugly a**. He would make all my demons come to life. Some demons I didn't realize lived inside of me. He brought the entire worst out of me.

I didn't know how to not let him get under my skin. Under my skin until that point, I didn't want the skin to touch my own body. The more he inflicted on me I began to realize this is not the way a husband is supposed to treat his wife. I wanted more, but I felt trapped. I had nowhere to go, no one to turn to. He felt like I needed him, he once told me that he made me and who I was at that moment. The joke was on him. My Creator is the Lord, for HE is my everything forever and always.

Have you ever given someone the power to think they made you?

Have you ever been in the dark while in a relationship?

Are you in the dark in a relationship today?

BEING ALONE

I've always felt alone; especially when my favorite cousin wasn't around me, we did everything together. We were glued to the hip most of our young years. He was one of the favorite kids in the family. He was my oldest auntie's son; we were two months apart, we did so many things together, he taught me how to ride a big wheel, he helped teach me how to drive, he and my very best friend taught me how to ride my bike; they were so much more advanced than I was, but they never left me behind. Anywhere my mom would take my siblings and me, my cousin was right there with us, he was really like my brother, and I was the sister he never had because he was the only child. These are our younger years it was always something going on in our house most of the time and all we had was each other. As we got older, I started to realize that my favorite cousin was getting more things in life than I was, and I mixed getting material things with getting love and compassion and happiness; boy was I wrong. He was just as lonely as I was.

As a child with so much going on inside your home and so many people living with you, it's sad that you can't get the proper attention that's needed to make a child feel complete. I remember I was in grammar school, and I needed some help on how to spell some things, so l picked up the phone and called one of my friends who was on my cheerleading team. I didn't feel comfortable enough to ask all the damn people in the house because they never had the time to show me anything, they yelled or cussed me out and told me to sit down somewhere. As my friends were helping me spell things you could hear her laughing at me with the people that were with her in the background; that was it for me it seemed as if I couldn't get help from anyone; this helped turn me into that person that God had to deliver me from.

My aunt gave me the name P-Lady; which stands for Pretty Lady, but everyone that came across me and heard that my name was P-Lady started calling me piss-lady or saying "Pee lady, pee in the bed". This went on for years and I had to defend myself all the time. I knew what it meant, but to be bullied all the time, it made me meaner and meaner.

My mother used to tell us that we didn't need friends, that they were not good and sometimes they were no good; but you need friends in your life. I was never really taught how to be a friend, that is probably why I don't have many today. You need friends, you need someone to lift you up and encourage you when those times in your life seem unbearable.

I got married for the very first time in my life at 23 and I was so very lonely looking for love in all the wrong places. I didn't know or understand who I was or to whom to belong. It's not healthy to create a life with others while being lost, let alone bring other lives into the world.

When being in a lonely state one must be very careful not to fall into that thirsty person; because when you become that thirsty person, you'll let anyone in and around you and that could be dangerous for you.

When I was married to my children's father, I thought we would have a wonderful life together, and boy was I wrong. From before the time of marrying him the signs were there, I just didn't understand them. He was a recruiter in the Marines, and he used that title to be the biggest whore I'd ever met. He was never home with us, and it was always because of work, that is what he would say, but I found out later he was living all kinds of lives everywhere with everybody. I would cook dinner for us and we would try and wait for him to come home so we could have dinner together and after it would get later and later, I had to feed my babies and put them to bed and he would come home after the kids were in bed most of the time or just too late to be bothered. It went like these the entire twenty-five years we were together. I would be up wondering " How did I get here?". Like, I knew I deserved better; I just didn't know how to get out of what I had gotten myself into.

I would be home many nights up wondering where he is; is he okay, has anything happened to him? Is he coming home? I remember one season of my disaster I was up asking myself, who is he chasing now, or who is he laying up with now? I wasn't wise enough to know that I'm a young girl under him, he got me right where he wants me like a little puppet in the house wondering where and what he's doing, while he's out doing exactly what he wants to do. But when that time came that I was wise, I was a force to be reckoned with.

Every time we had some type of gathering my so-called husband at the time would never be a part of it as a family. He would always have to come alone or with some other nothing of a man, he had to show up as if he was the star that everyone was waiting to see. This made my skin crawl more than anything at the time. When he walked in the door; he would want everyone to call his name and run up to him as if he was God himself. Believe it or not, he use to tell everyone in my family to call him God. Everyone laughed at him and made fun of him all the time. I was always annoyed with him thinking he was as great as God. He had nothing on my Lord, God!

As a child, being alone isn't good. You have all kinds of thoughts when you are alone and have no one leading you to make good decisions for yourself. You go out into the world thinking your thought process is good or on point for making a good and conscious decision, then you find yourself in some situations You don't have the strength to live in.

BEING ABUSED

There are many ways of being abused and I've experienced some if not all of them, I do believe. It all started with the way I was raised. In our home. I was being talked to in ways a child should never have been spoken to. I was taught to be abusive to other people especially the elders in the house; they were the target of being picked on by the younger ones in the family you see, I watched my uncles and aunts be abusive to their aunts and uncles and you know you are a product of the company that you keep and at that time in my life they were the only company that I kept so I learned a lot from them.

My mom was very abusive; but again, you are what your environment makes you until you understand for yourself that this is not normal and learn how to create your own normalcy. That was something my mother never learned to do, unfortunately (may her soul rest in peace). She was very mean and angry most of my life when it came to raising her children (the first three anyway). She wasn't a communicator and if we did anything to piss her off in any way whatsoever, she would beat the crap out of us. She had no patience for us, her patience consisted of being knocked across the room with marks left to prove it. It never took much to tick her off.

Can you imagine having your one and only parent being so abusive to you?

Where do you go?

Who do you turn to?

After my mom got pregnant with my oldest sister, life changed for her in more ways than just becoming a parent, she pretty much lost all the support she thought she had. Her Father disowned her completely. She had to leave us in that house with everyone that didn't care ENOUGH about her to make sure that her children were well taken care of. When I say well taken care of; I mean by being talked to with love and understanding and not being cussed out, showing favoritism to the other children that lived there as well, teaching her children how to do their schoolwork, and being patient with her children. Her two older children's father was very abusive to her; so, you see how her pain and abusiveness trickled down to her children? She gave us what he gave to her. She was left alone to figure life out all by herself, which followed me for most of my life. I was really messed up because of this abuse that started with my mother's life.

I used to get whipped for anything. I received black eyes and much more. I thought this was the way to be a parent. I took this abuse into my parenting; it was the only way I knew how to parent until I was so abusive to my son, I hurt myself (emotionally) in the midst of being abusive to him. To put that type of abuse on him. I started to cry out to God and begged him to help me with my children; because I love them too much to hurt them/him in this way, and something said to me (I say now that; that was the Holy Spirit)! Start having a conversation with him. I started having conversations with him and things got better from that point with my child abuse.

When you are being abused in your home; you tend to allow other people to abuse you as well most of the time unbeknownst that it's happening. It was so easy for me to be a target for my first Husband to come in and be very abusive to me. I loved him and he abused me in every way he could. This was normal for this is what I watched in my home as a young girl; my aunts' men fought them all the time and I saw it and they stayed with the men through the abuse. It was mostly women in our family, the men were not taught how to be real protective men, we the women protected the men in the family. I blame my grandfather for that, he was a typical nothing of a man who was fighting his own addictions. He was a drug addict that didn't know how to be a real man to the family he created; instead, he was this man that brought this curse of being abusive to his family.

My grandmother was a very strong woman when it came to keeping her family together, but very weak when it came to showing everyone how not to be so abusive to one another and maybe she didn't have the knowledge on how to do that and her pride wouldn't let her seek out for something different than what she knew to do.

My grandmother was a loving grandmother, I understand now more than ever that she did what she could at the time. Maybe if she wouldn't have had favorites of her grandchildren and we all had been treated equally, we probably would be better off today showing compassion, understanding, love, and support because we act like foreigners from another country or island, we don't act like family at all.

I pray every day that God fills me up with everything like him. It's not painful in his presence and I love being in his presence!

Some people don't get to escape from their abuse.

Are you one of those that's still living in your abuse?

If so, what are you planning on do about it?

When I imagine myself being a wife, I never thought I would be an abused wife. When I say abuse, I mean it in every way that word spreads.

Physical abuse is the worst, people could see the way I was being hit, slapped, slammed and kicked. Whatever was being inflicted on me I was wearing it out loud. I remember he blacked my eye to the point I couldn't see out of it, there were flashing of white light in my eye for weeks. I went to the ER, but I didn't stay, I didn't stay because I was too ashamed for anyone to know, even the people I didn't know; I stayed in that room for weeks. People would come to see me, and I wouldn't allow them to come in the room and I wouldn't come out, my cousin came to visit one day before she got upstairs, I asked My ex-husband's mother to tell her I was taking a bath and I was going in to the bathroom like I was in the tub, she told me yes but when my cousin got upstairs my mother-in-law told her EVERYTHING. I didn't know she had told her so I was in the bathroom pretending like I was in the tub in hopes that she would leave. She didn't leave for a while, trying her best to get me out of the bathroom so she could see how bad my eye was. I found out later that my mother-in-law told my cousin EVERYTHING, my cousin went right and told my family, who I was trying to hide from. My stepdad sent for my ex-husband and for some years I didn't have a problem with him putting his hands on me, I have no idea what was said because when I asked my ex-husband, he told me it was nothing. That nothing gave me some peace for a while, at least with the physical abuse the verbal and mental never stopped.

Can you walk away, when you know you should walk away in that moment?

Do you know how to walk away?

Mental abuse has you in a dark place for however long you're being mentally abused, it turns you into this evil and angry person.

Verbal abuse makes you lose all confidence in yourself. Words hurt so bad.

BEING MENTALLY CAPTIVE

I never thought I'd be there in this place for so many years of my life. I literally was mentally captive by someone who thought I was a joke, someone that had no respect for himself let alone me. This man had me so fixated on being together and trying to make our family grow and be better than we have ever been before; by always telling me one thing and then doing something totally different so, here is why I was all by myself.

It's like down in this state of mind; I know I'm sinking; I know what I don't want to know but hoping for the best. I mean I was stuck here; I couldn't move no matter how hard I tried. I was getting weaker and weaker but still holding on to something that wasn't healthy for me.

Why on earth was this happening to me; I just wanted to be loved back. I wanted him to feel what I was feeling but he never did, and I stayed, Man did he have some hold on me that I couldn't escape from? The more I wanted; the worse it got. I kept trying and trying. When you think and have hope that it can and will get better you put in all the over time until there is just no more time to put in.

Trying to sleep at night but you can't; because you're up wondering "Where is he? Why hasn't he come in yet? What could he possibly be doing at this hour?". You start calling his phone but guess what, there's no answer! My heart would hit the bottom of my gut with every call I had to make and no answer.

One phone call to my surprise; he answered the phone, only so I could hear him making love to someone else. All I could do was stare into space as if I was a part of it. I'm so deep in this at this point I'm insane.

I would try to have conversations about the incident that was at hand. When I tell you he would turn things on me and made it all my fault. He would get so mad call me out my name, get in my face, head butt me, hit me, and the list goes on. I would fight back, but this wasn't my fight to win, this was the Lord's fight. I learned that later in life.

His sister would hook him up with her friends and tell me what he had going on with them; took me over to one of the friend's house and while we were there she goes in the room with the friend (you know to tell her who I was); while they were in the room the friend starts to talk out loud about what her and the ex-had been up to lately. As I was listening, I got more and more upset. I told my sister in law "I'm leaving" so then they wanted to follow me back across the street and I couldn't take it anymore, so I unleashed the lion on her friend. My foot got caught up in the long coat that she was wearing, and my ex-mother started shouting "GET HER FOOT FROM UNDER THERE"! This was a whole mess. A mess that I endured for years.

It's like my mind was in a slave mode for love, love that never existed, a love that was a bet from the very beginning, a love that was lost before it was even found. I was mentally in bondage holding on to pure air falling deeper and deeper into my own destruction waiting for someone to catch me; only to find no one there. Always trying to figure things out, only to find me right back at the beginning and always giving in to the problem.

The problem always seems to be someone else's until you learn to take accountability for your own actions in a situation.

One time my ex-husband took the credit card from me knowing we didn't have food and we needed some household goods for the house.

I had to call one of his superiors in charge. He made him give me the card back and told him if he ever took it again, he would be in some deep trouble.

While sitting here in this state of mind making all the wrong decisions with my children, it was constantly on my mind how to get out. Sometimes, while moving in this dark space you are oblivious to what's going on around you, and in the end, you all suffer.

Being in love is unpredictable, you must be careful about how you fall in love and to whom the individual may be. Love is magical, we must take care of our mental state in this area, it is very important. LOVE IS INTENSE! We must be careful with our motives. Love is incredible. We must follow instructions from God!! Love is everlasting, if you build your foundation by putting God first.

I only wanted to be in my bubble at this time in my life, I thought everyone would see what I was going through by just looking at me.

One time I went to visit my ex-husband while he was serving time in the federal jail (That's another story to tell) and the whole visit he was confessing his so-called love for me, telling me how when he got home he wasn't going to allow his sister's in our marriage anymore, no more listening to them it's just me and you, me and you. You know how you want that to be true, but deep down inside, you know it's not; everything he has ever said to you has been a lie. Why would this be different?

He proved to me that I was right, he came home and was in the same act of hot-mess-ness and I was trying to get away, only this time FOR REAL!

Have you ever given in to a problem, only to find yourself right back where you started?

Do you always take the short end of the stick?

Are you aware that you're being abused during any period of your life?

BEING NAÏVE

Every time someone told me they didn't mean it, or I took it the wrong way; I believed them and welcomed them to do it all over again because I was too naïve to see people firsthand, I never knew what that meant. I really had to go through a lot of heartache in my life for being so damn naïve about situations, people, places, and things.

I allowed so much to go on in my life because of being naïve; so many useless relationships. I always went into a relationship with the expectation of longevity the only thing I went into with longevity, and no one else was interested in the same thing as I was. I didn't know about boys to men, only having intentions of getting one thing out of a relationship and that was sex, once they get it they're out! Man; that is the most heartbreaking thing to go through; but I kept on and kept on repeating this pattern over, without understanding why I kept landing there.

I didn't really understand how a relationship was supposed to work. I always wanted to be in a relationship because I thought that's where all love begins; Boy, was I wrong. Love really begins from your foundation, in your home. Love is so kind and understanding and it shouldn't hurt but when you come from a bunch of hurt individuals winging life with no real tools; anything is liable to happen. I guess for many years I was winging life without any real tools; I was a product of my own environment and didn't understand what that meant while living in it. I never thought my family was as dysfunctional as we were until I got out and got into another family that was worse off than mine on so many other levels of life.

I remember once in high school I was liking this guy I thought was cool! He must've thought he was as cool as I did because he played with my emotions in that way; he knew I liked him and wanted to be with him. We exchanged numbers and used to have conversations on the phone all the time, but when we were in school, he wouldn't show me the time of day. For quite some time I continued to keep something alive with us by continuing to call and show him interest. I had to s swallow whatever that was that was stuck in my throat and told him to push on with me being the chaser; I didn't like the feeling of chasing this boy and not getting the attention I thought I should get so l stopped with no understanding as to why I am landing there in the first place.

There was no real communication in our home. I didn't really know how to express myself for a very long time.

When I got married. I would confine in his baby sister; we had become tight, more like sisters than the other two sisters that I was close with. I would share what her, what her brother and I were going through, and she would share what her and her husband was going through. The difference between the sisters, she (the baby sister) was in the service. She showed me to never get too close to a snake. She betrayed me to be my friend/sister, but it was like she was getting information and taking it to him they would plot against me. The more she found out I had been close with her other sisters she would turn evil on me, and this went on for years until I said enough is enough.

I was always there for people who always had an agenda to hurt or use me in any way. I always thought I needed to have people around me, I never understood what that was all about until I needed more than just people being around just for their own good. I didn't understand giving all of myself to people that didn't deserve it.

People will destroy you if you allow them to. You must understand WHO you are.

Do you know who you are today?

49

BEING ON AN EMOTIONAL ROLLER COASTER

Sometimes I didn't have a clue as to what was going on around me. My emotions have always been all over the place. I knew how to express one emotion very well and that was anger.The next would have to be confusion because only the Lord knows how confused I was and, making decisions in a confused state only gets you higher and higher on that roller coaster, so high sometimes you can't see anything because of nausea that was leaping up from your stomach. Sometimes I would have to swallow that nauseating feeling and keep it moving, no one could ever see this side of me, who would understand? Who cared enough? Who do I have? Where am I going?

I had to figure something out but first I had to get a hold of myself. How do I do that? I have no education, I have no skills, and I have no tools whatsoever. What was I good at other than loving all the wrong people? I did nothing but cry this entire season of my life. I could never have a solution to a problem, I just couldn't focus. I started to doubt my entire being. I needed my mom; I needed some help. I watched everyone live a happy life all around me and I was miserable in my own skin. I started to not like myself; every time I looked in the mirror, it showed nothing, nothing but a fool that was ashamed of myself. There was nothing pretty about what I was looking at. Uneducated, and, an embarrassment of my own self.

I could sit in front of you and be so far away from you at the same time. I was never living in the present time; I was always searching for understanding. I've never met anyone like my ex-husband and his family; they were something fierce in my life, they played so many mind games and kept you in so much foolishness. They weren't a family that operated out of any kind of love whatsoever. Their dysfunction was something different than mine; I was always on guard around them, and you just never knew what was to come. They would steal my money and then act as if we were the best of friends. They would team up against with me a lot of times, but you better believe I always stood my ground with them.

It was four sisters that I really spent my time with; one of them was a natural-born hater for no reason that I ever understood. On our wedding day when the Pastor asked for you to speak now or forever hold your peace. She yelled and asked him if, he was sure; the whole entire church got quiet and he uttered the words to say, "IT'S ON" and my cousin then shouted "It's on" like you don't want this smoke. What a way to start a marriage off? He never defended me when it came to his family, I had to fight all of them off me at any given time. One holiday my then-father-in-law took the whole entire family out for dinner and this same sister had a hissy fit about me going. She started a big commotion about it; and my then-husband said nothing, he just kept walking around the house like nothing was being said or anything was going on. I couldn't believe what was happening; I was so down on myself at this time I kept letting this chick have her way until enough was enough. Now I'm in a defensive mood. I'm turning into something more and more unstable than I saw coming.

Every time someone would come around, this sister would tell a bunch of lies about me turning everyone against me. This sister hated me but would always come begging for my money when she needed something. When out-of-town folks would come to visit, as soon as this sister realized that they liked me in any way, she would start a bunch of lies about me making it very uncomfortable for me and the visitors. Therefore, it is very important to love yourself even when no one else loves you, you must be comfortable in your own skin.

LIVING INSIDE OF MY OWN EMBARRASSMENT

Can you imagine living inside of your own embarrassment? Well, this is how I lived for many years. I didn't know who I was. I didn't know how to comprehend enough to get myself from one side of town to the next. I couldn't comprehend how to not fight for something that was so invisible right in my face. I couldn't stop chasing those people, places, and things that kept me from being able to breathe on my own. I couldn't stop allowing the same hurt to re-enter into my heart, I just couldn't stop that from happening repeatedly just enduring someone else's life pain all on me. I couldn't escape that; because it was embedded in me from my roots, they inflicted the very first heart pains in my life and it just kept going and going, until I called on Jesus! How wonderful he is!

I learned how to hold things in and live with a deep dark Secret like I couldn't read, or I have very low self-esteem and I'm ashamed to be around people who I feel that I'm just as or even more intelligent than. I kept things like this inside a dealt with them in a way that I knew how which made me angry and defensive all the time.

I was pretty but felt dumb as a doorknob. If a conversation arose and I felt like I was losing comprehension I would remove myself from the situation and would dare anyone to question why I moved the way that I did, that was that defense mechanism that I carried on my back for years. I was scared for myself at one point. I would get so angry that my skin would start to burn badly, and I would want to tear someone's head off; I knew I was losing it at that point, and I had to get some help quickly.

I would wear flannel print clothing all the time. I had no sense of style. I always wore everyone else's clothes. When I was in grammar school, I used to wear my mom's shirts to school and, one day my childhood friend called me out on it in a joking way, but that tore me to pieces that he even noticed. I was so ashamed. My oldest sister used to have all kinds of stylish clothes and one day I must have put these red pants on; they fit well, and I felt good in them. I was on the front porch one day and the neighbors were out there with us as they usually are. The neighbor friend looked me up and down with this funky kind-of look on her face and said out loud in front of everyone "Why do you have on my pants"? I looked at her and spoke? "First of all, these are my sisters." But on the inside, I was so ashamed to be put on blast like that in front of everyone; so, I ran in that shell I was building for myself.

You can live inside of yourself only until you can't anymore and then and only then is when your help will come; no matter what no one tells you, when you are sick and tired of your own embarrassment is when you'll start to think differently, then your thoughts become your reality, you have to move in a positive light even when the time gets rough because they will. Never give up on yourself!

Sometimes I would go around with my friends and have nothing to offer to the conversation or substance of life. I would listen to them have happy lives with their families and husbands, and I wanted that so bad; I would always ask God, what did I do to suffer like this, I have so much love in my heart, I just want to be loved. I'm a good daughter, sister, wife, and mother, but I keep falling short on this life journey. I would ask, how long do I have to endure so much pain? I wanted to give my kids such a different life, how could I do that living with so much pain?

I lost two babies; they both had the sack but no fetus inside the sack. That blew my mind and took me a very long time to get over it, I had a son and wanted another child so he could have someone to grow up with. I didn't understand at the time the why and that's why I went to an even darker place in my life. To make matters worse my husband jumped me while I was recovering from the miscarriage, my mind was all over the place at this time; I was away from everything I've ever known trying to create something amazing with all my enemies (my ex-husband and his family). I still had to figure out how to be a mother too and for my son, not realizing I had him around everyone and everything that would make his life a living hell including his father.

I've never been on my own and away from my roots although I was willing and ready; I wasn't ready for what was ahead. I was moved right to my ex-husband's playground; all his hoes were there waiting on him and the family was there to help him make it all come to life in the presence of his wife. One time I was coming through the hallway of his nephew's home where everything went down and, one of their friends were coming through the door which was a woman, the men was watching some music videos on the television and my ex said to the friend I could be the one that but that one you, pertaining the videos on the television; she smiled and said "Don't you have a wife'? As he was going to answer he turned and looked me dead in my face with a smiley face, and of course when I go off and do a scene, I'm the one creating drama, the story of my life.

Sick people always blame and hurt others…

When people used to tell me I'm a drama Queen, it would automatically take me to an angry place and make me defensive. I didn't want to be looked at as a drama queen. To me being a drama queen, means I bring nothing but conflict to someone's life. I always felt like no one understood where I was coming from. Then I realized it wasn't that no-one didn't understand me, they just didn't take the time to be there for me.

Sometimes asking the right questions will give you an understanding of the individual's characteristics and give you an understanding as to why they're acting or moving in ways that look suspicious.

We could never get him to do anything with us as a family. Husband, or father he just wasn't into us as a man should be into his family. I felt like I failed my children. This man is their father, and he doesn't want to spend any time with them; to show our son how to be a man. I didn't know at the time that he couldn't show my son how to be a man, he was failing big time in that department. It is more to being a man than just going to work and bringing in a paycheck. What about quality time, having those one-on-one talks teaching them about this mean ole world, what ever happened to being a caring Dad for your child, and not making life all about yourself?

I had to live with the fact that this is my husband, I had to learn how to detach myself from his way of living, and how my children were living inside of this bubble of lies, deceit, dysfunction, cheating, and all kinds of abuse. I have missed out on a lot of people, places, and things placing myself in such a destructive way of living, trying to love someone who's worse off than I could have ever imagined.

I never knew how bad off we were until we got out and tried to live a normal life, with the tools of being abused, neglected, and walked all over. We realize there's work we must do individually and as a whole family.

You must do the research and spend the necessary time with an individual before you make a sound decision on letting them into your life, and then create a family with 'em, it's crucial to your well-being. I was ashamed to call myself his wife, it didn't sit well in my soul and that's not how a wife is supposed to feel in her marriage.

Have you ever had to defend who you are?

Are you still defending who you are?

SLEEPING WITH THE ENEMY

I never thought getting married and having a family would've ever been a nightmare of a lifestyle for me. I've always envisioned something completely different and loving with a little bit of floating from time to time. It was everything but loving, in fact, it was one of the worst experiences in my life. I never for a million years thought that I would look at my husband at the time as an enemy, but that's exactly what he was. He was never kind to me, he just put up with me because when you're truly in love you are kind to one another, love shouldn't ever hurt and this love that I was getting from this marriage was very painful.

This was a red flag that flew right over my head. One day my husband (at the time), one of his friends and I were sitting in his room. I was sitting on the bed with the friend in a chair, and the husband at the time was standing, he moved over to where I was sitting turned himself around in front of me shook his butt and farted in my face. He started laughing as if he had just hit the biggest comedian scandal. I was furious! And all his friend could do was shake his head in disbelief and this was only the beginning of my nightmare of a life.

I didn't really have a foundation that I could look up to when it came to marriage or even relationships; for I didn't have that in my home. I knew that I wanted a marriage and children. I wanted a man that would be good to us and be proud and happy with the foundation that we were building together. I thought that I could have someone who could hold a conversation without hitting me because I disagreed with something. I thought I would be the only woman in my husband's love life, but I was the last woman he thought of every day. I thought where I fell short, he would lift me up, instead, he stomped on me and laughed about it. I had to listen to my husband at the time talking to his sister on the phone and he called me all types of B****es and dumb a**. I had to hear this on the regular. I used to defend myself, but I came to understand after so many attacks that the behavior would get more and more intense.

My husband (at the time) would look me in the eyes and promise me a bunch of lies and I kept hanging on to the promises and not paying attention to the actions because the action always revealed the true liar he was. On our wedding night, we were to get a bridal sweet downtown until we could plan for our honeymoon that never happened. He brought all his friends from out of town back to our one-bedroom apartment and told me he wasn't leaving his boys, and we were all there on my wedding night talking about the military. On our first-year anniversary he was supposed to be taking me out but, some chick that was supposed to be a cousin needed him to take her and her husband to rent a car. He told me it would only take thirty minutes to an hour, and he'll be right back for our date, it was more like eight hours later. When he got back, he acted as if everything was normal. Every question I had; he would shut it down if I poked too hard, then I would become the punching bag for the night; this went on for years.

I would find nasty dirty underwear of other women in my husband's skate bag, and naked pictures of women, and if or when I confronted him about everything got turned around like I had caused the wrong that was at hand. There was never peace in this marriage. I always wanted more than I was getting and had hoped that God would fix it and turn everything all around towards a fresh start, but every time things would get worse. I remember one time while living on base one of the military wives, a friend of mine caught hold of who he was on IM, so she started a relationship with him over the internet, this is when instant messenger was a thing. She would IM him; they would flirt back and forth, she asked him if he was married, and he told her "Yes, I'm married, not dead", my heart fell to the floor without anyone seeing it happen.

One year for Christmas, I go into our bedroom to get something and I see his phone light up; I go over to see who was trying to get through because we were having our family over and to my surprise, he was having a whole conversation telling some woman about how he couldn't stand me and my family, how he couldn't wait to get away from us. I didn't say anything to anyone, I just accepted the fact that I don't know who I'm sleeping with anymore.

I remember one time my son and I had been home all day waiting for the man that's supposed to hold us down and protect us. He had created this lifestyle of leaving home from sunup to sundown for work as a recruiter in the Military. When I would ask about these hours, he would tell me that's a part of recruiting; and sometimes it was but not as often as he was using it for. That night I guess I had too many questions and he hit me, and I hit him right back. We fought in front of our son, and he body slammed me, I fought back until he rammed my head into the wall right over my son's bed. From that incident alone I have this permanent stain on my front tooth. I always thought the stain came from drinking coffee until the dentist asked me if I ever had any head injuries.

There would be plenty of times he would buy himself a thirty-pack of his favorite beer, and he would drink half of the thirty-pack. Halfway through that, he would turn into this raging monster that went through the entire house tearing us down in any way he thought of. I would defend my children before I would ever defend myself. I knew someday I would get us out of this I just didn't know when or how. There have been plenty of times that I thought I would never see light again.

There was this time when my ex-husband picked up our son and myself from my grandmother's house and as we were walking down the stairs to get to our car, he saw his ex-girlfriend in the car with someone else; he politely walked over to that car with our child and I'm following like a fool and when we got closer to the car she jumped out, hugged him and said a few things to our son. Not one time did he introduce me to her or acknowledged me as his wife.

When we walked away, I was thinking, how rude? When we got into our car, I asked him who was she? He told me her name and right away I knew who she was. I asked why didn't you introduce us? He couldn't answer that question. That's how a lot of our conversations went. I never got a straight answer. I don't think I ever got the truth out of him.

I would always ask myself. How did I get here? I knew I deserved better than him, I felt trapped more times than not. I would ask myself over and over"Why I love him so much?" because what he was showing me wasn't love, respect, compassion, or understanding. How could I give myself to such a person? Did I think of myself as worthy? I couldn't have.

Every weekend was party time with my ex-husband. He made sure he didn't miss whatever was going on and I was never a part of the festivities. I asked him. Why do you have to go out every weekend? He told me because I work five days a week and the weekends are mine. My eyes got so big; my stomach dropped a little out of my body. I couldn't believe what I was hearing, I mean what about us and our family? Everything I had in mind as to what a family was supposed to be, I Definitely didn't get that. I thought we would be able to take our children out on family trips, to the mall, and teach them about being human beings and how to manage relationships, emotions and all the things that come with life. I had no understanding of who I was sleeping with because this person was no husband of mine. I always had to make sure that my children and I were protected. His family knew he was destructive and just set back and watched the show, the show of tare down Latrice and her kids, and make it look like she is the problem and that's exactly what they did blamed me and my children for his sickness and all the bad choices he was making as a man of our family.

One year I purchased a vehicle and I needed to get some insurance for the car, so I called our insurance company, USAA. As I was explaining to the agent the type of insurance that I needed, he told me that he should call my husband to ask for permission to give me this insurance. I said, "Excuse me, I'm his wife; I'm on the policy as well and I just called the other day taking care of something else, are you sure?" He said, "Yes ma'am your husband called and changed everything, he says you guys are in the process of getting a divorce?" I said "Oh really? I didn't know that; that's news to my ears." I asked if he could call my ex-husband so I could see what was going on and he said, "Yes, sure, I sure can," and he did just that. When the ex-husband got on the phone, he said, "Why do you need my insurance ? Get your own." I said to him, "Are you serious, you called these people and told them to take me off the insurance that we're getting a divorce and you haven't talked to me about it?" He said "How long you're going to need to be on it, because you only have 6 months and then you must find your own." I said "WHAT? UNBELIEVABLE! You have got to be kidding me." I was lost for words.

The agent goes on to say " Don't worry ma'am I can still take care of you, nothing changes; you'll just have your own policy now and you won't have to go through your soon-to-be ex-husband." WOW! I was blown away; I couldn't believe what I was sitting in at that moment.

One time our cable bill was due so I took a check to pay the bill. I'm sitting at work and my son called me to tell me the cable was not working, I said "What do you mean not working, I just paid the bill ! Let me call to see what's going on". I called the cable company, and they told me that my ex-husband had called them and told them to reverse the check. I said, "WHAT? You can do that? I said are you sure? Why would he call and tell them to reverse the check, this is his house we live here together." I called him to ask about the check and he told me "Yes, I did. I didn't tell you to pay that bill, use your own money to pay that bill". Once again, I looked dumb in front of my children, he shut the cable down for no reason. Just because he had that power didn't make it right.

There have been so many times my ex-husband would see me out in public and wouldn't acknowledge me as if I was none existence to him. I loved him so much that I was blinded from doing the things I needed to do for myself. I couldn't understand at the time why he couldn't love me back, but today I understand that hurt people hurt people and how could he ever give me any kind of love when his home was full of confusion, misunderstanding, abuse, and most of all family secrets that they would all take to the graves with them. When you don't know who you are or what type of damage you're dragging alongside you, you are no good for yourself let alone anyone else. It's very important that when you recognize that something isn't right with you or the things around you, don't be afraid to get some sort of help.

CHANGING THE WAY YOU THINK

Everything starts with a thought, you think it, you do it. You think it, or you don't do it. Which one you choose to do is the outcome of some situations ahead. You must be careful in the way you think and how you sort things out in your own mind. Don't stay in thought a too long and lose the sense that it makes. Once you lose the sense of the thoughts in your mind everything starts to come all together as one thought and you start to lose your power of having control over your thoughts. Then you become combative, defensive, and maybe even start to misplace situations and everything becomes one.

When you change from having a bad thought into having a good thought, your outcome will be amazing. You can keep thinking one way and moving in a different way, which means your movements are not aligned with your thought process, and you need to rethink things and try moving in the order of the thought that's going to put you in a positive state. This doesn't happen overnight; it's a process and you sometimes must sit in that process until God is ready to elevate you to a higher level of life.

Sometimes while in a trancelike mood and your thoughts are moving faster than you can keep up with, to sort them out. You should snap out of that mood and refocus so you will be able to put your thoughts together, sort them out to make some sort of sense, put the new way of thinking in order, then turn your order into action, and start yourself on a journey of freeing self from the Chaos that's inside your head.

Don't ever think you can think of someone else, because the thoughts that you are having about them in your mind, could and most likely be wrong about that person. You must take the time to get to know someone before you can tell them about themselves, because the thoughts that are in your mind, it's just your thoughts and not necessarily reality.

Overthinking can cause you to make some bad decisions for yourself, sometimes we take an overthought and put it into a situation, causing the situation to be worse than it needs to be. Take your time, gather your thoughts, and make them make sense to you. Don't be afraid to ask questions to make sure you're not being damaged by the situation.

Don't be afraid to apologize to anyone that you have caused some discomfort because of your overthinking. Once you start to practice these tools of changing a negative into a positive thought, you'll see a big change in your everyday conversations, decisions, and the way you move.

When you are thinking things through, don't allow yourself to get stuck in that one thought for a long time, it could become damaging.

Have you ever been stuck in a thought?

How long is too long to be stuck in a thought?

When do you ask for help, when you are stuck in a thought?

Who can you trust your thoughts with?

You can always trust God with your thoughts, and everything else of yours!

For a long time, I had no one with whom I could share my thoughts with. So, I held them to myself, and it built anger inside of me, the more I kept it to myself, the worse that anger got. When I learned how to give every thought that came to mind, to my Lord and savior Jesus Christ, that's when things start to change and make more sense.

When you can take some time out for yourself to do some self-reflection, you can really see things differently, and where the root of all those unworthiness issues come from, and start to sort them out and make changes wherever is needed, and watch how you grow.

Plant a seed in your mind with positive things that you want to accomplish in life, set goals to make those accomplishments come to life, and water your seed every single day. You must do something every day towards your goal, it doesn't matter how small that thing you do towards your goal, just don't sit around and expect things to start to happen. FAITH WITHOUT WORKS, IS DEAD!

You must encourage yourself daily. Everyone doesn't see your vision the way you see it, stop trying to convince them. Tell yourself"I can do this, I will make it, I'm powerful, I'm smart, I'm a winner"! Whatever it is you need to feed your mindset to keep you on a positive journey do it, and be selfish about it, you can't be good for anyone if you're not taking care of yourself first.

No matter what you are going through be able to make a conscious decision and make sure you understand what you're deciding on in the matter.

Have you ever made an unconscious decision?

Did the unconscious decision make life harder for you?

Did you have to get help after your unconscious decision?

Raising my children, I thought I was doing everything right. I thought all the decisions I made for them were good decisions. When I found out later in life that some of the decisions that I had made for our family, for good, turned out to be not so good and made my children live a different life.

I made some decisions that I may not have made if I were in a clear headspace and thinking on my own, by not letting the things that I was going through influence my thought process while in the moment of making decisions. Never lose focus! It's important that you take your time and make good decisions while not in a good head space. It's also important that you build a strong foundation of communication with your family/children, make sure everyone is on the same wave line, get the understanding as to why and why not, make sure everyone is getting their point across, and everyone should get an understanding as to what is or what could take place for the family and then make the final decision after that.

COMMUNICATION

For many years, I thought I had the communication tool down pack. I knew I had a lot to say and I thought I was delivering it in the right manner but as the years went by and I met more and more people, I quickly learned I was doing it all wrong. When it was first brought to my attention that I had insulted someone by expressing myself, I got even more defensive because who was going to tell me how to let them know how I feel, or how they were making me feel? I had to learn the hard way to watch how my delivery was.

Coming into our home, we didn't always get corrected when saying something wrong. I didn't understand I was saying things wrong until I got around people to make me feel bad for saying things in the way I was saying them. People can make you want to hide yourself and if you can't handle someone telling you about yourself, in a way that is correctable to your state of being it could make you lose who you are.

I love to communicate, I love to ask questions, I've always been that way. People would make me feel bad because I ask a lot of questions. I feel like it's a gift from God. I said that because I've learned that some people won't ask the very question that they need the answer to the most. I come to understand it takes a lot of courage to ask a question, so I'm thankful that God has given me the ability to ask questions.

I thought I was communicating well during my first marriage. We both didn't have this tool from our home foundation to be brought into a marriage in the first place. He was the leader of our family, so he set the tone for how things would flow, and the way he communicated was physical. When someone puts their hands on you, in return you must let them know to never do that again, no matter how many times it took place. when you realize the harm, it does to the ones around you, you cry out for another way to communicate and understand that you must be patient with yourself when having a conversation with others, no matter how much you hear something about yourself that you don't like, you must hear it all before you can say anything.

If you don't know how to communicate, please learn how, it could be the make or break of your life. If you go into a relationship with no communication tools, you're setting yourself up for a failed relationship.

Teach each other how to speak and be spoken to. When we can't express ourselves, we become misunderstood, or we think to ourselves that no one understands us and, what are we doing wrong. It's ok to not know, but don't be afraid to ask questions.

There are many ways of communicating; you have good communication, bad communication, misunderstood communication, etc. You must learn where the person is who you are having a conversation with and communicate with them right there, even if you feel like you're lowering your level of communication. It's ok. You both will understand what's going on with each other.

Another important factor in communicating is being a good listener. If you don't hear everything that's being said, you can't have an adequate answer. Sometimes if not most, we listen to defend, sad thing is the majority of the time we don't have to do that at all, all we must do is just listen to get some understanding. This was a battle for me for a very long time, I had a point to prove; but to no one but myself. I would never listen to what was being said in a conversation before I would respond and would be totally off what was being said, all because I was being a hothead and had to get my point across. This happens when you are around people who don't listen to you and always talk over you when you're just not a factor in one's life.

Today, I communicate with an open mind of understanding, I listen to be of help or maybe even get some help somewhere in my life on my journey. I've learned over the years; I can have a conversation with a child and learn something new at that moment, and that excites me to be able to get some knowledge from the future to be. It makes me proud of that child!

I'm learning to be different from my younger self while evolving into this woman of movement, to inspire young to mid to older women to live inside of their worthiness and not settle. Let them know that it's okay to not be okay sometimes, we just can't stay in that not-okay space and let it take over us. No! We have the power within us, and we must learn what that power is and where it's rooted from.

Do you have good communication skills?

Are you a good communicator?

Do you allow a person to finish the question before you answer?

I've been through a lot in this life of mine. I had to learn everything on my own, and I'm still learning to this day, I will forever be learning something new, something different. I have made so many mistakes in life, and I have learned a great deal of life from those mistakes, some I had to repeat over and over again just to say to myself, 'I GOT IT! I try my hardest to not make the same mistake twice these days in life, It's not everlasting here on earth, so as I can learn and grow and teach, that's exactly what I'm going to do.

ENDING

I discovered that I love to write. I love to put my thoughts on paper and then read it to myself, sometimes the words make me cry, sometimes the words make me laugh, and sometimes the words take me into such a deep thought and make me want to dig deeper into the why, or what, or who, or when, and to get to the root of what's being presented in my thoughts.

I'm a Woman of God! I'm so proud to say that because for years I've been running away from that part of me and trying to live and fit in places that I was never meant for me to be. I've always felt different, just didn't understand that side of me. It's a seed that's been planted by my biological father's mother. I love everything about this side of myself, deep down in my soul I'm connected to God! If I had known about this side of me in my younger years, I would have tapped into it then, and maybe, just maybe things would have been different. Here or there, I had to go through everything I encountered. I'm a strong Woman of God because of it all.

I've discovered that family brings strength. I'm learning to accept everyone in my family just the way they are. I've learned my experience is my experience and no one wants to hear what I have to say, and that's okay, I still love them all. I can't change the things from the past, but I'm learning every day how to move forward in Love. There are times when I need to go around the elderly in the family just for that pick-me-up, the ole fashion style; but these days you have to take what you can get and be happy with that.

God has always been there when I thought I was all alone, he was right there waiting for me to connect with him and be filled with the Holy Spirit. Being filled with the Holy Spirit is a whole different level of living, and I'm appreciating it daily, as well as learning to live in it. Thank You, Jesus for this wonderful gift. I love to learn God's word, it's very fulfilling and will forever change my life. I'm so thankful that he kept his hands on me, and still walks with me every day.

For years, I felt like I was in prison, trapped and couldn't get away when or how I wanted to. I never thought I would be sitting here writing this book about how down and out I've been for the majority of my life. I never thought I would find someone to love me, with all the damage that came with me. BUT GOD!

I'm so thankful to God for my purpose of being here on this earth.

I made up my mind that I needed more than what I was putting out, and more than what I was receiving so I had to make some changes. I put myself in an online school to get my high school diploma, and when I tell you it wasn't easy, it was not easy. I had to teach myself everything I was running away from, which was education, learning how to read and comprehend what I was reading. When you don't know a lot of words, you tend to stay away from the reality of using big ones that makes you look foolish trying to pronounce them. It took me a while to finish. I got stuck on that math; it took me three almost four years to realize that I didn't need that math I was taking. I had to choose another subject, which was literature, a form of English that was my favorite subject. I raced through that literature, sent in my work, passed every one of the courses and my diploma was in the mail, thank you James Madison High! People would always try to correct me when they thought they knew my story, to tell me I have a GED, NO! I HAVE A HIGH SCHOOL DIPLOMA, THANK YOU! GET IT RIGHT... I was very proud of my accomplishment, and I wasn't going to let anyone dismiss my WORK or WORTH! I did that all on my own... Understand the journey before you dismiss it.

While I have accomplished this goal, it build my confidence a little more; made me want to know more about myself and how much I wanted to take this education that I had got to another level, so I was like; let's see what you got. I went to College for Business Accountant; please tell me why did I do this to myself. This is what I kept saying after the class started because before I started, I took the assessment tests to see if I could even get into the school, I passed this test to my surprise. I'm a horrible test taker, my nerves get the best of me every time, and I start to shake, it's weird but that's what I go through, so when I passed the exam; my excitement was above the sky, my confidence was even higher. This is exactly what I need in this moment of my life, and today I'm grateful for that experience. After I passed that assessment test, I was so excited went home to tell my family, and when I got there, I went into my son's room as I opened the door, that dog was in his room, we made eye contact and he came chasing after me and attacked me, I fell, broke my wrist and this had ruined my surprise for my family (there's more to this story).

I have learned over the years that I'm worthy, deserving, loving, kind, considering others, sometimes more than they consider me. I'm beautiful, and I'm smart to name a few of my own acknowledgments. Thank You Jesus! I couldn't have realized these things about myself without you.

I have learned how to think and make decisions on my own. I know how to manage my homework and everything that comes with it. I couldn't do this without asking for help, now I'm the help! I love being able to help others. The help for others, showing someone how to be better than yesterday, or the moment before I started to help, is rewarding within itself. Thank You Jesus!

I was working as a housekeeper some years ago, and I was surrounded by the majority of CNA's so I got to see firsthand what their work consisted of. In my mind I said I would never do the duties of a CNA, and now I've been doing this CNA/Caregiver for over twenty years now and I love it. I have made a career out of it as a private caregiver, providing love and compassion to the elderly those who are in need at the time of their services.

You can tell God what you won't do, and he'll show you just who's in charge. Laughing at us while we're making our own life plans. I'm tapped in connected to the source and letting him lead and guide me along the way.

As I learned new and improved things about myself. I realized I was helping others in a different kind of way. The things that I would say were very uplifting, encouraging, inspiring, and just plain motivating. I learned that I love doing this. The feeling that I get when I'm helping, but most of all the outcome from it all is very exciting! I enrolled in a Life Coach Class and became a Life Coach. I'm so grateful to be able to show others how to bring out what's already there, but for some reason, they can't see it until they start their own process. The joy it brings me when someone has come to understand their full worthiness.

The way I have connected with God is unexplainable. I say that because every time he shows up and shows out, rather it's big or small, I'm always in ahh! I always try to explain what he has taught me, but others always seem to don't understand what I'm talking about or just don't want to hear what I have to say. I'm filled and being filled every day, I'm so grateful for his unchangeable hand on my life.

I have always had big dreams. I have always wanted to live in a nice big house in the suburbs because I was from the city of Chicago and I lived in a two-flat, that was owned by us for us, but it didn't always feel that way. My mother didn't move out on her own until I was in high school. I just always wanted more, and now I can make that happen for myself. I have my education, I can read much better than I ever could, I'm writing books, I'm married to someone who loves me unconditionally and we share similar life obstacles. There are a lot of things I haven't experienced in life, and neither has he so we get to enjoy exploring together. He's a friend and a lover that I didn't imagine ever having in one person, I've won in this area of my life. I can finally say, I'm happy!

Being in love is a wonderful feeling, especially when your partner loves you just as much or maybe even more. The love is magical, and nothing could break it apart, you withstand what seemed like the impossible, but you do it, and you do it together. What a wonderful feeling! I love it here.

Everyday, I'm striving for perfection within myself. I'm comfortable in my own skin and it feels fantastic to be here. I had no clue where I was headed before I tapped into my calling, and now I can't rest without trying to figure out how to make someone as well as myself bigger and better than we have ever been before in our lifetime.

I enjoy spending time with my grandchildren, they light up my life to the full capacity. Each one of them has a beautiful yet different personality. They are the reason I strive to be healthy. They bring a different kind of joy to my life.

I pray that they'll always remember how deep my love is for them. It is different when your son gives you grandchildren, versus your daughter giving you grandchildren, it's like you go through hell

just to love what's rooted to you by your blood, but what can you do but have faith and hope for better days to come. I'm a loving grand-mother and will go to the end of the earth for my babies. I never knew being a grandmother would have you on cloud nine just thinking about their precious little faces, and all the things you get to experi-ence with them, and then you get to send them back to their loving parents. WOW! As soon as they're gone for a good twenty minutes, you start missing them and start calling their phones asking them when they are coming back, because you miss them already. I love it here!

As you grow in life, you learn to do things differently. You learn that you've made mistakes and when those circumstances come back to haunt you again, you have better tools on understanding how to move differently, or just say something in a different way, or have a better tone. I've learned how to use this tool and I'm able to be a different kind of parent to my grandchildren, something that my kids will learn over the years. Sometimes when you are trying to explain something to others if they're not in a listening season of their life at the moment you're trying to give them some sort of knowledge; you have to meet them where they are and be okay with what's transpiring in front of you.

We don't always get the tools we need before we're put out in the world to swallow us down and leave us at the bottom of the ocean with our eyes wide open shut, trying to figure out how to get out of there without completely losing what's left of oxygen in our mind, body, and soul. All you can think of is get me out of here, someone, anyone, help me, I'm losing it. Before you know it out of nowhere, here he comes to save the day. The Lord will always be there to pull you from the bottom of that ocean. He will fill you up with all the oxygen you'll ever need, just trust and believe in him.

Have you ever been at the bottom of the Ocean?

Are you at the bottom of the Ocean now?

Where are you in life today?

Who are you showing up for in life today?

In our family, we were taught how to use our tongue in the worst kind of way. We got to express ourselves; meaning defending ourselves and being very sharp with our tongue, to the fact it taunts our family today. Sometimes members will say anything that comes to mind, thinking it's funny when it actually tears a person into pieces, especially when they're trying to live with a different formula that is healthier for them. You try to teach one, but you can only teach one when one is willing to learn. Don't live in darkness all your life, if someone is giving you some wisdom, or knowledge you should take it, it's part of maturity, maturing in life along your journey.

I'm a Life Coach, my Practice is Empowerment of Self Worth! Today, I want to empower you to live in your full worthiness. Self-reflection can and will get you moving forward in life. Free yourself from that thing that keeps you stuck, confused, and nowhere to go.

I was freed from my old ways of thinking. I put myself in a foreign way of living, thinking I had to have others' approval to do whatever it was I wanted to do. What was I thinking? This is how bad my self-esteem was, couldn't do anything without anyone's opinion about if it was good or bad or if I should do it at all. Those days are over with, I know who I am, where I come from, and most of all who and what generational attachments I have which give me a total understanding as to why things played out the way that they have in my life, and give me even more reason to keep this fight alive on my journey to help another recover from the bondage's that's been brought into their lives.

I want to thank each and everyone that took some time out of their busy lives to read about mines, and how I have overcame some really trying times in my life. When God calls you to do something, you may not understand how things are playing out in your life, but if you continue to stay connected with the Lord, he'll reveal everything to you in due time, HIS TIME! Just hang in there, and stay focused; that's the main part, staying focused. Don't let the noise around you affect what God is instructed you to do through the Holy Spirit. I had to learn how to be obedient to the Holy Spirit. When you are so used to doing life in your own way, you have to learn how to do this in a new and better way. I'm growing and learning everyday.

Thank You Jesus!

I have been working on other books as well as this one. I never thought in a million years I would be putting my life in words for others could understand that they're not the only one's out there that struggle with obstacles, and trying to figure out how to get from underneath that rock they allowed themselves to fall under, or fallen into the bottom of the ocean trying to figure out how to come from underneath it, and still have some sense of dignity in life.

This was very therapeutic for me, I didn't realize how much I needed to get all of this out of me, I feel so refreshed, my life is starting all over, and it's not easy, but it's worth it! You know how you have that feeling, that I've finally got it together, first with God, then myself, my children are on a road to their own healing, and doing a fantastic job on their journey. I'm so proud of them, for what they were giving in life; they are becoming more and more successful in their own right. I Love them forever and always all through eternal life and beyond.

Coming Soon:

My Truth

The Bet!

Did you win or Lose the Bet?

The End!